Soaring to New Heights: Career Transitions for Pilots and Cabin Crew

by Princess Duncan

Dedication

To my father, Prof. Samuel Ato Duncan, your exceptional support and incredible wisdom have been the foundation of my journey. You are not only a remarkable father but also an inspiring teacher whose guidance has shaped my path in ways I cannot fully express. Your unwavering belief in me, your endless love, and the countless sacrifices you've made are beyond words. I am truly blessed to have you as my father, and I will forever be grateful for everything you have shown and taught me.

HRM Otumfuo Osei Tutu II, I am profoundly thankful for your constant blessings, prayers, and enduring support. You are an outstanding king whose contributions to humanity and our nation are unmatched. You are a mentor and role model, and I follow your example with the utmost respect and admiration.

To my mother, Joyce Mills, and Aba Docia, your lasting love and invaluable advice have guided and shaped me into who I am today. I am immensely grateful for your wisdom and care. And to my family, the Ninety-Nine Women Pilot, and my dear friends, I am forever thankful for your love and encouragement. Your support has meant the world to me.

About the Author

Princess Duncan is a visionary leader whose extraordinary journey bridges multiple industries. As a highly Cadet Pilot training in the United State of America, entrepreneur, and Deputy Chief Executive of one of the largest medicine manufacturing companies, she embodies both leadership and innovation. Her rich background in cabin crew training, paired with her degree in BA (Hons), allows her to seamlessly blend aviation expertise with sharp business acumen.

As a Queen Mother, Princess Duncan upholds a deep sense of responsibility and compassion for her community, making her not only a leader but a figure of inspiration. Her diverse experiences, intelligence, and creative vision make her uniquely qualified to share insights that will resonate with aviation professionals and readers worldwide. Her extraordinary writing, coupled with real-world ideas, ensures that her work will leave a lasting impact on all who read it.

Contents

Chapter 1

Understanding Your Current Situation

Assessing Your Skills and Experiences

Let's be real, assessing your skills and experiences is one of those things that sounds a bit boring at first, but it's crucial when navigating a career shift, especially in the aviation industry. Whether you're a pilot eyeing management, a cabin crew member exploring new roles, or an aviation pro dipping a toe into entrepreneurship, knowing what makes you *you* is essential. Take a moment to reflect on your experiences. What have you learned during your time in aviation? Identify the competencies you've developed, such as technical skills, customer service, crisis management, and teamwork. Spoiler alert: these things seriously boost your market value.

Now, don't just focus on the professional stuff. What about those personal qualities that make you stand out? Are you the kind of person who can stay cool under pressure while everyone else is losing their minds? Maybe you're a natural-born leader or a smooth communicator. These soft skills are just as important as technical knowledge and can greatly enhance your employability in various fields, whether within aviation or in a new industry. Highlighting them not only boosts your confidence but also gives you a better idea of what new career paths are calling your name.

If you're stuck on where to begin, try using self-assessment tools. Tools like personality assessments, skills inventories, and reflection exercises can help you gain deeper insights into your capabilities. You can also ask colleagues, mentors, or even a life coach for feedback. Sometimes, they'll notice strengths you didn't even know you had (who knew that solving in-flight meal crises was a transferable skill?). Gathering this intel will give you a well-rounded view of what you bring to the table, which is super handy when you're polishing up your resume or prepping for interviews.

Now, let's talk gaps. We all have them. Maybe you're lacking a certain certification or need to brush up on some skills. That's totally okay! It's all part of the process. Being honest about where you need to improve shows that you're committed to growth, not that you're weak. This may involve pursuing further education, obtaining certifications, or even seeking volunteer opportunities that can help you bridge those gaps. Recognizing these areas for growth is not a sign of weakness; rather, it reflects your commitment to personal and professional development. Embrace the mindset that every bit of progress counts, even if it means going back to "student mode" for a while.

As you compile your skills and experiences, remember that it's not just a boring list. This is your professional *story*. Every turbulence, smooth landing, and in-flight drama has shaped your journey. Sharing these experiences with potential employers or clients can make you stand out. Presenting yourself authentically will build trust and spark interest. Each experience, whether a challenge or triumph, adds depth to your profile. Trust in your abilities, stay proactive in your development and approach this transition with confidence. The sky is not the limit; it is just the beginning of new horizons waiting to be explored.

Identifying Your Passion and Interests

Finding your passions and interests is a crucial step in any career shift, particularly for those who have spent years in the aviation industry. Let's face it: the thrill of flying through the clouds often makes you forget about your personal goals and dreams. Now's the perfect time to hit pause and reflect on what truly excites you beyond the cockpit or cabin. Think about activities that make you lose track of time or fill you with energy and enthusiasm. Whether it's a passion for teaching, an interest in health and wellness, or a desire to explore entrepreneurship, recognizing these elements can help guide you toward a more fulfilling path.

Start with some self-reflection (grab a pen, or maybe just your favorite playlist). Jot down your hobbies, interests, and the things that light a spark in you. This exercise isn't just about listing things you enjoy, but also about uncovering the underlying values and skills you possess. For instance, if you find joy in helping others, it may signal a future in life coaching or wellness support. Similarly, if problem-solving in aviation excites you, roles in aviation management or consulting might be worth exploring. Your unique experiences in aviation provide a solid foundation for new opportunities.

Now, let's talk people. Start chatting with others who've taken the leap and made career changes. Networking can open doors to insights and experiences that may resonate with your own journey. Attend workshops, webinars, or local meetups focused on career development and growth. Engaging with like-minded individuals not only broadens your perspective but can also spark ideas on how to integrate your passions into a new career. Pro tip: every conversation is a chance to learn and can potentially lead to your next step forward.

And hey, don't be afraid to experiment! Dip your toes into

different roles or volunteer in areas that catch your interest. Trying things out hands-on is a low-pressure way to see if a certain career path is right for you. For example, if you're thinking about becoming a health and wellness coach, offer a free workshop or start creating content online to see how it feels. This kind of trial run not only builds your confidence but helps you zero in on what really clicks with you.

Finally, keep your confidence strong along the way. Career changes can feel like venturing into uncharted territory, but don't forget to give yourself credit where it's due. Your aviation background has armed you with transferable skills like teamwork, communication, and problem-solving, things any industry would be lucky to have. As you identify your passions and interests, remember that each step you take is a part of your growth. Accept the adventure of discovering a new path, and trust that your experiences will lead you to soar to new heights in your career.

Recognizing Challenges in Transition

Changing careers, especially in the aviation world, can feel like deciding to skydive without double-checking your parachute. You know it's going to be a rush, but there's that moment of *oh no, what have I done?* For pilots and cabin crew, moving away from the familiar skies and into a whole new role or industry brings a cocktail of emotions: excitement, sure, but also the kind of nervous energy you get when the seatbelt sign turns on and you're still in the bathroom.

The good news? You're not alone in this. Realizing these feelings is the first step to getting through them without pulling out your hair. Every career switch comes with its own set of turbulence, whether it's emotional (hello, imposter syndrome), professional (learning new jargon), or personal (saying goodbye to your favorite airport lounge). But recognizing these bumps in the road can actually help you stay on course and keep you motivated. After all, you didn't get through those red-eye flights without learning a thing or two about navigating tough situations!

One of the most common challenges people face when switching careers is the fear of the unknown. Yep, that pesky "what if" question can send even the bravest into a spiral of anxiety about new responsibilities, adapting to different work cultures, or starting from scratch. For aviation professionals who are accustomed to a structured environment, stepping outside their comfort zone can feel like flying blind. But here's the thing: embracing that fear as a natural part of the journey is how you take back control. Instead of letting it freeze your progress, face it, and remind yourself that it's all part of growing.

Another big challenge? The potential loss of identity. For many pilots and cabin crew members, their careers are not just jobs, they're a huge part of who they are. So, when they shift into a new field, it can leave them feeling disconnected from that sense of self. It is important to recognize that while their roles may change, their skills and experiences remain invaluable assets. Highlighting the transferable skills acquired during their time in aviation can help individuals rebuild their confidence and redefine their professional identity in new contexts.

Of course, no career change should be a solo mission. Support systems are *gold* when navigating this transition. Whether it's through life coaching, peer groups, or mentorship programs, surrounding yourself with people who've been there, done that can offer both comfort and practical tips (and maybe a reality check when needed). Connecting with others who've successfully made similar leaps can give you a peek behind the curtain of what's to come, along with a healthy dose of motivation. And let's not forget about coaching that boosts your confidence and self-esteem, because sometimes, you need someone to remind you that you've got what it takes to ace this new chapter.

And let's not forget that stress is a loyal companion during any career change. It shows up uninvited and makes itself right at home. Managing that stress is key to keeping your sanity intact. The emotional toll of change can increase stress levels, affecting both mental and physical health. That's why it's important to lean on stress-busting tools like mindfulness, exercise (even if it's just a walk around the block), and healthy habits. These small choices can do wonders in keeping the stress monster at bay. Prioritizing self-care and reaching out for professional support when needed can help you tackle this transition with resilience and keep your eyes on the prize.

Remember, every bump in the road is just another chance to learn. With some grit, a clear game plan, and a solid crew backing you up, you'll be climbing toward new career heights in no time!

Chapter 2

The Power of Mindset

Cultivating a Growth Mindset

Cultivating a growth mindset is like finding a hidden superpower when you're navigating the ups and downs of a career change. It's all about believing that your skills and intelligence aren't set in stone, they can grow with some good old-fashioned effort, persistence, and a dash of resilience. This mindset can be a real game-changer, especially for those in aviation, where job loss, industry shake-ups, or personal setbacks might feel like hitting turbulence. By embracing a growth mindset, you'll start seeing challenges not as roadblocks but as opportunities to learn, adapt, and level up. And before you know it, that mindset will be the fuel that helps you take your career to new heights.

For parents of future aviators or current aviation professionals, nurturing a growth mindset in their children can give them a solid runway for success. Encouraging curiosity, problem-solving, and resilience when the going gets tough helps young individuals build the skills they'll need in an industry that's always evolving. Parents can model this mindset by sharing their own growth and learning experiences, emphasizing that setbacks are merely stepping stones toward greater achievements. This supportive environment nurtures confidence and self-esteem, making it easier for the next generation to pursue their dreams in aviation.

Entrepreneurs and agents within the aviation sector also stand to benefit from a growth mindset. In a competitive market, being able to adapt and think outside the box can make all the difference. By embracing change and chasing new opportunities, you'll not only stand out but lead the way. Industry shake-ups? No problem. Those aren't roadblocks, they're springboards for new strategies and growth. And when you take this proactive approach, not only are you leveling up your own career, but you're also giving others a reason to follow your lead. Why not inspire those around you to adopt the same mindset?

Government officials, you're in a prime position to shape a culture of growth within the aviation industry. By pushing initiatives that encourage continuous learning and development, you'll be helping aviation workers feel supported, and trust me, a supported workforce is a happy one. Programs, mentorships, and wellness resources can make all the difference. When leaders at the top model a growth mindset, it sends a strong message to the whole industry: *We've got your back*. And when people feel that, they're more likely to embrace change and thrive in it.

Finally, for those engaged in coaching, whether in life, career change, health and wellness, or stress management, instilling a growth mindset in clients can be transformative. Coaches, you're like the personal trainers for people's minds. You can help them spot those sneaky limiting beliefs and swap them for empowering thoughts that fuel their growth. Whether it's teaching stress-busting techniques or confidence-boosting exercises, your guidance can make all the difference.

Overcoming Limiting Beliefs

Conquering those limiting beliefs? Yes, that's a must. Self-doubt and those nagging, negative thoughts can often prevent professionals from realizing their full potential. These beliefs show up as fears of not being good enough, worries about job security, or just plain old anxiety about chasing new opportunities.

Recognizing these uninvited thoughts is the first step to kicking them out of the cockpit. Once you've spotted them, you can start reclaiming the confidence you need.

So how do you tackle these limiting beliefs head-on? Start by reflecting on the mental stories you've been telling yourself every time you think about changing career paths. Is there a little voice saying, "You're not qualified enough," or "What if you fail?" Write them down and analyze their origins. Where did these thoughts even come from? Often, they're hand-me-downs from past experiences or societal expectations (thanks, world). Understanding their origins gives you the power to challenge them, rewrite the script, and start believing in your potential.

Remember, your thoughts shape your reality, so why not tell yourself a story where you succeed?

Visualization is like your secret weapon for smashing through limiting beliefs. Seriously, picture yourself absolutely *killing it* in the role you want, whether that's moving up the ladder, jumping into a new field, or even launching your own aviation business. Close your eyes and imagine the skills you've honed, the knowledge you've built, and the rock-solid network of colleagues cheering you on. This isn't just some feel-good daydream, it's a confidence-boosting exercise that reminds you just how capable you are. The clearer you can paint that mental picture, the more real those aspirations become. It's like giving yourself a sneak peek into the future, where you've already won. And guess what? The more you see it, the more you believe it, which makes stepping forward with fresh determination feel natural.

Surrounding yourself with the right crew makes all the difference when you're tackling a big career shift. Find mentors, peers, or even life coaches who get what it's like to navigate the ups and downs of the aviation world. Sharing your fears and aspirations within a safe environment fosters encouragement and accountability. These connections can provide valuable perspectives and insights, reinforcing the idea that you are not alone in your journey. Plus, their success stories can serve as proof that the possibilities ahead are real, not just wishful thinking.

And don't forget to be kind to yourself along the way. Seriously, self-compassion is like your co-pilot when it comes to overcoming limiting beliefs. You're bound to hit some bumps and moments of doubt, but how you handle those setbacks is what truly matters. Celebrate each small win as progress toward your goals, and treat every challenge as a learning experience. Remember, every successful pilot, cabin crew member, or aviation entrepreneur has faced obstacles of their own. By cultivating a resilient mindset and focusing on growth, you'll be well-equipped to leave those limiting beliefs behind and take your career to new heights.

Harnessing the Power of Positivity

Harnessing the power of positivity is like adjusting your compass, it keeps you on course through the complexities of career transitions. The journey can be filled with challenges, not exactly a walk in the park, but having a positive mindset can be your secret sauce to success. And no, positivity isn't just about feeling good all the time. It's about rewiring how you view obstacles, seeing them as part of the process rather than roadblocks.

In an industry like aviation, where change is practically the norm, staying upbeat can really keep your momentum going. For pilots, cabin crew, or anyone itching for new opportunities, the trick is to focus on what could be rather than what's in your way. Think about it: aviation management, training, even starting your own venture, there's a whole runway of options. By keeping your outlook positive, you'll find that every transition is a chance to experiment and grow. Who knows? You might just stumble into your next big adventure while you're at it.

Positivity also plays a major role in supporting your health and well-being during times of change. Career transitions can crank up the stress levels, and that stress doesn't just hang out in your head, it can mess with your body too. That's why practicing positive self-talk, keeping a gratitude list (yes, even on tough days), and surrounding yourself with upbeat people is like giving yourself a break from the pressure cooker. By creating a positive bubble around yourself, you'll fend off a lot of the anxiety and uncertainty that come with change. You'll be able to face challenges with a clearer mind and a lot more patience. This shift in mindset is beneficial for you and can inspire those around you, fostering a supportive community in the workplace. After all, positivity is contagious.

Harnessing positivity is also about building self-esteem and confidence. As you embark on a new career path, it is easy to succumb to self-doubt, particularly in a competitive field like aviation. However, celebrating your achievements, no matter how small, and acknowledging your unique strengths reinforces your sense of self-worth. This practice can empower you to take bold steps forward, whether you are applying for a new position, pursuing additional training, or launching your own business. Your belief in your capabilities can act as a powerful motivator, driving you towards your goals.

The ripple effect of positivity is far-reaching. Your outlook can shape not only your own path but also the experiences of those around you. By modeling a positive mindset, you help cultivate a culture of encouragement and support within your professional community. This shared sense of optimism can drive collaboration, innovation, and collective resilience, ultimately helping everyone to reach new heights.

Chapter 3

Setting Clear Goals

Defining Your Career Aspirations

Defining your career aspirations is like plotting your course before takeoff. It's essential for reaching your destination, especially in a fast-paced field like aviation. Whether you're a parent, pilot, agent, entrepreneur, cabin crew member, or even a government official, understanding what you truly want from your career can fuel fulfilling experiences and remarkable achievements. So, let's take a moment to reflect: What really lights your fire? What's driving you? This bit of self-awareness isn't just for meditation. It's what sets you on the path to career satisfaction and success.

Begin by envisioning where you see yourself in the next few years. Close your eyes (not while flying, please) and picture your ideal role. Are you leading a team? Developing the latest aviation technology? Mentoring the next generation of high-fliers? Whatever it is, jot it down, and dream big! Even if your aspirations feel as far-fetched as developing a jetpack, write them down. These goals will serve as your career compass, keeping you aligned with your purpose. And remember, it's never too late to redefine your path; every step you take toward clarity enriches your journey.

Have some conversations with mentors or peers who've gracefully navigated their own career transitions. like getting advice from a co-pilot who's been through a bit of turbulence but still landed smoothly. Ask them about their challenges, victories, and those pivotal decisions that shaped their journey. You might just pick up a few gems of wisdom that spark your own ambition. Plus, networking within the aviation world can open doors to hidden opportunities you never knew existed, kind of like discovering that secret first-class lounge.

As you fine-tune your career aspirations, think about how they fit into the bigger picture of your life. Balance is key, after all. If wellness and personal time are important to you, look for roles that won't keep you grounded in burnout. Passionate about coaching? Find ways to weave that into your aviation career, whether through mentorship or teaching. Aligning your career with your personal values will make everything feel a little more, well, *in sync,* like an autopilot that just gets it.

Now, to keep you from aimlessly drifting through the clouds, set yourself some SMART objectives: specific, measurable, achievable, relevant, and time-bound. Break those lofty dreams down into manageable steps, and celebrate each little victory (yes, even the small wins count). Having a structured approach will keep you focused and motivated, even when turbulence hits. Embrace the process of defining and pursuing your career aspirations, as it will not only lead you to new heights in your professional life but also empower you to inspire others in the aviation community.

Creating an Action Plan

Creating an action plan is like building the flight path for your career transition. It's essential for getting from point A to point B without feeling lost. Start by reflecting on what you want from your future, whether in aviation or beyond. Write down your goals, whether they involve advancing in your current field, transitioning to a new role, or even exploring entrepreneurship in the aviation sector. Getting this clarity will give you the confidence to move forward.

Once you've nailed down your goals, it's time to break them into smaller, actionable steps. This method reduces the sense of being overwhelmed and gives you the opportunity to celebrate each milestone along the journey. For instance, if your goal is to secure a new position, outline the necessary steps: updating your resume, networking with industry contacts, and researching job openings. Each task completed brings you closer to your ultimate objective and reinforces a sense of accomplishment, boosting your confidence as you progress.

Adding a timeline to your action plan is crucial for keeping up the momentum. Assign yourself realistic deadlines for each task, nothing like a little pressure to keep you accountable! But keep it flexible; life likes to throw in a few unexpected detours. Use planners, digital calendars, or whatever tool keeps you on track to visualize your progress. Marking key milestones and deadlines creates a sense of urgency, driving you to stay focused and overcome any obstacles that arise.

Support is another important element in creating an effective action plan. Engage with mentors, coaches, or peers who can provide guidance, encouragement, and accountability. Sharing your goals with others not only helps you stay committed but also opens doors to invaluable insights and opportunities. Surround yourself with a crew that's got your back. A supportive network creates the kind of positive atmosphere where you can really thrive, allowing you to draw strength from the shared experiences of others in the aviation community.

Also, remember to regularly review and tweak your action plan as needed. Career transitions are anything but static, so staying adaptable is key. Celebrate your achievements, learn from setbacks, and refine your strategies to align with your evolving goals. By maintaining a flexible mindset and embracing change, you will not only navigate your career transition successfully but also soar to new heights in your professional journey. Your action plan is not just a set of tasks; it's a powerful tool that can elevate your career and empower you to embrace the future with confidence.

The Importance of Short-Term vs. Long-Term Goals

Setting both short-term and long-term goals is key if you're serious about growing in your career. Think of short-term goals as the small, manageable steps that keep you motivated and moving forward, one win at a time. These little victories are what boost your confidence and help you stay proactive. And honestly, it's those small steps that keep you grounded, especially when you're dealing with the unique challenges of a career in aviation. They give you something tangible to focus on while you work toward the bigger picture.

On the other hand, long-term goals are what give you that broad, inspiring vision for your future. These are the dreams that let you picture where you want to be in five, ten, or even twenty years. Whether you're working towards a leadership position, considering new roles, or even thinking of stepping into entrepreneurial ventures, long-term goals serve as the guiding compass that informs your day-to-day decisions and keeps your bigger purpose in focus.

Balancing short-term and long-term goals isn't just a strategy. It's a lifesaver, especially when it comes to managing stress. Let's face it, big dreams can feel overwhelming, but breaking them down into smaller, manageable tasks takes the pressure off. Short-term goals give you those bite-sized wins that make even the loftiest ambitions feel more achievable. This approach fosters a healthier mindset, allowing aviation professionals to thrive in high-pressure environments while maintaining their mental and emotional health.

The balance between short-term and long-term goals also builds resilience, something we all need, especially in a fast-paced industry like aviation where change is a constant. Setbacks happen, but having short-term goals in place acts like a safety net during those tough times. They remind you of the progress you've made and what you're capable of, even when things don't go as planned. This resilience isn't just a professional boost; it spills over into your personal life too, helping you handle challenges with more confidence.

In the end, appreciating the value of both short-term and long-term goals helps you take control of your career and personal development. By setting realistic, actionable short-term objectives that align with broader aspirations, you create a powerful roadmap for success. Accept and appreciate the journey, celebrate the small victories, and stay focused on your target.

Chapter 4

Building Confidence and Self-Esteem

Strategies for Boosting Self-Confidence

Self-confidence is such an essential part of thriving in any career, and in high-pressure fields like aviation, it becomes even more crucial. Confidence doesn't just help you perform better; it strengthens communication and teamwork. One way to build this confidence is by adopting a mindset that embraces challenges and sees failures as learning opportunities. It's also important to set realistic goals and celebrate small wins along the way. These little moments of success can really help boost your self-esteem and give you the push you need to keep growing in your career.

Another great way to boost your confidence is by always learning something new. Whether it's through formal training, workshops, or even self-guided study, gaining new knowledge and refining your skills can help you feel more capable. In aviation, the more you learn, the more prepared you'll feel when faced with challenges. This also shows your colleagues and employers that you're committed to doing your best. The more skills you build, the easier it becomes to trust in yourself and what you bring to the table.

Positive self-talk and visualization can also work wonders. Try changing your inner dialogue by replacing any negative thoughts with affirmations or supportive statements. And visualization, imagining yourself succeeding, can help reinforce a positive mindset. These techniques help create a sense of readiness and confidence that can make tackling new challenges feel less intimidating. Reminding yourself of your past wins and the skills that got you there can also give you the motivation to push through new obstacles.

It's also really helpful to have a strong support system. Surrounding yourself with people who encourage and uplift you, whether they're mentors, coaches, or just positive peers, creates an environment where you feel supported in both your personal and professional growth. Having that network to share experiences with and get feedback from can make you feel like you're not navigating this journey alone. Relying on others for support during tough times can really help maintain your confidence, especially when transitioning through different stages of your career.

Taking care of your physical and mental health through regular exercise, good nutrition, and mindfulness practices can really boost how you feel about yourself. When you feel good physically and mentally, it's easier to show up confidently in your work. Stress management techniques like meditation or deep breathing can help you stay calm, too. By looking after yourself holistically, you build a solid foundation for confidence that can carry you through your career with ease.

Embracing Your Unique Strengths

Let's be honest: career transitions can be challenging, especially in an industry as dynamic as aviation. But here's the good news, recognizing and embracing your unique strengths can be your secret weapon as you move forward. Whether you're a pilot, cabin crew member, or aviation professional, understanding what sets you apart is key to boosting your confidence and finding clarity during career shifts. And yes, we all have those unique strengths, even if it sometimes feels like your main strength is just making it through a day of flight delays and packed schedules.

It all starts with a little self-reflection (don't worry, no therapy session required). Take a moment to think about your skills and experiences, both in aviation and beyond. What tasks do you consistently excel at? What aspects of your job do you find most fulfilling? Engaging in this reflective process helps you identify the qualities that set you apart from others in your field. Maybe you're the problem-solver everyone turns to, or you have a knack for connecting with people and easing tense situations. These strengths are not just assets; they are the building blocks of your professional identity and can guide you toward fulfilling career paths.

Once you have pinpointed your strengths, the real progress happens when you fully accept and own them. This means not only acknowledging what you do well but also allowing these qualities to shine in your daily interactions and professional endeavors. If communication is your thing, take on leadership roles in team projects or mentoring. If you excel at managing under pressure, step up in situations that need a calm head. By using your strengths every day, you not only enhance your career prospects but also create a more positive, collaborative environment for those around you.

Now, aviation is a field full of surprises, and career stability isn't always guaranteed. But here's where embracing your strengths really comes into play, those who know their strengths are more adaptable. You'll find it easier to shift into new roles or even pursue entrepreneurial paths because you have a solid foundation of self-awareness to rely on. Instead of seeing change as a setback, you'll view it as an opportunity to apply your strengths in new ways.

Remember, this whole "embracing your strengths" thing isn't a one-and-done deal. It's an ongoing journey. As you grow in your career, your strengths will evolve too. Stay open to feedback, try new things, and don't shy away from asking mentors for their perspective. Keep building on what makes you awesome, and you'll not only survive but thrive in whatever comes next.

Celebrating Small Wins

Career transitions can feel like climbing a mountain, and the summit sometimes seems impossibly far away. But here's a little secret: celebrating the small wins along the way makes that journey feel a whole lot more manageable. These small victories, even the tiniest ones, are like mini-milestones that keep you motivated and remind you that progress is happening, no matter how overwhelming things might get.

Think of them as checkpoints. Whether it's acing a training module, landing an interview, or just surviving a week of navigating your new role, these moments deserve a little fist pump. And don't underestimate the power of a cheer squad, whether it's your parents, partner, or friends giving you that extra boost, their encouragement can turn a small win into something worth celebrating. These celebrations remind you that every little effort is moving you closer to your ultimate goal, and that's a pretty great feeling.

The cool thing about celebrating small wins is how it can totally flip your mindset. When you start focusing on what you've already accomplished, rather than stressing about what's still left to do, it lifts a weight off your shoulders. Suddenly, the mountain you're climbing doesn't seem so daunting. Instead of getting bogged down by the challenges, you start seeing the journey as a series of rewarding steps that make the whole process a lot more enjoyable. It's amazing how a little shift in perspective can melt away stress and build up your resilience in the face of uncertainty.

That's why coaches are big on celebrating small wins. It's not just about ticking boxes, it's about learning to value the progress you've made. Coaches help guide their clients to recognize these moments, boosting self-esteem and helping them stay focused on their goals. When you start owning your small victories, you'll feel more in control of your journey. And trust me, that confidence rubs off on those around you too.

At the end of the day, celebrating the small stuff is a habit worth picking up. Whether you're an aviation professional making policy changes or an entrepreneur navigating the ups and downs of building a business, those little wins matter. By creating a culture where small victories are acknowledged and celebrated, you foster a sense of community and encouragement. And that collective celebration? It not only uplifts individuals but also strengthens the entire industry. It's a win-win, really! Pun intended!

Chapter 5

Networking and Building Connections

Leveraging Your Existing Network

Leveraging your existing network is a powerful strategy that can significantly ease the journey of career transition. For pilots, cabin crew, and aviation workers, your network isn't just a list of people you've shaken hands with, it's a treasure chest of relationships that can unlock new doors. Your former colleagues, mentors, and industry contacts? Yeah, those folks could be the key to landing your next role. So don't be shy. They can provide valuable insights into potential job openings, recommend you for positions, or even connect you with decision-makers in their organizations.

Now, before you think, "I don't want to bother anyone," let me stop you right there. Relationships, especially those built on trust and mutual respect, are meant to be leveraged! People in your network likely remember when they were in the same boat, and you'd be surprised how many are more than happy to help. Maybe it's a fellow pilot considering a move into a different role or a cabin crew member exploring entrepreneurship. Sparking conversations with them can bring clarity and ideas you hadn't even considered. Plus, a little shared venting never hurts.

In addition to seeking advice and job leads, consider how you can give back to your network. Networking is not a one-way street.

Offer your skills, whether through mentoring someone new to the field, volunteering for an aviation cause, or sharing valuable resources. Being generous with your knowledge strengthens your connections and shows you're still in the game, committed to the aviation community. It's like giving out good karma: what goes around, comes around. You help them, they help you, and before you know it, you've got a whole support system cheering you on.

Social media platforms like LinkedIn present incredible opportunities to expand your reach and connect with professionals outside your immediate circle. Join aviation-related groups, jump into discussions, and share your expertise with others. The more you engage, the more visible you become to potential connections who might offer collaboration, advice, or even job opportunities. By being active in these spaces, you position yourself as a knowledgeable and resourceful member of the aviation community.

Don't overlook the potential of networking events, industry conferences, and workshops. These gatherings are prime hunting grounds for new contacts and opportunities. Sure, walking into a room full of strangers might feel as nerve-wracking, but step out of your comfort zone. Approach these events with curiosity and a genuine desire to learn. Each conversation could lead to something you hadn't even imagined, and hey, you might even enjoy yourself.

The people you've met along the way aren't just a part of your past, they're a bridge to your future. Whether you're leveraging your existing contacts or expanding your reach, your network can help you take off to new heights in your career transition.

Expanding Your Professional Circle

When you step into the unknown, it's important that you ease that journey by expanding your professional circle. Whether you're a pilot, cabin crew member, aviation agent, or even an entrepreneur, building a solid network can unlock doors to new opportunities and offer much-needed support. The key is to approach networking with the goal of making real connections, not just treating it as a business card exchange. Every interaction is a chance to build relationships that can boost both your personal and professional growth.

Attending industry-related events and conferences is an excellent way to expand your professional network. These gatherings not only allow you to stay updated on the latest trends and innovations in aviation but also provide the opportunity to connect with like-minded professionals. Don't be afraid to introduce yourself, share your experiences, and ask thoughtful questions. You'd be surprised how quickly these conversations can lead to new connections, ideas, or even mentorships. Just remember to follow up with the people you meet! A quick message on social media or email can keep the relationship going and show that you value the connection.

Speaking of social media, platforms like LinkedIn are goldmines for networking. You can join aviation-focused groups, participate in discussions, and share your insights. Engaging with other professionals' posts or commenting on articles is a great way to start meaningful conversations. And don't forget, your online presence reflects your professional identity, so make sure your profile showcases your skills and passions. It's like your digital business card that works 24/7.

Mentorship is another powerful tool when expanding your professional circle. Finding a mentor who inspires you, whether it's a seasoned pilot or a successful entrepreneur, can provide guidance through the tricky parts of a career transition. A mentor can guide you through the complexities, share their experiences, and provide invaluable advice. But mentorship works both ways, consider becoming a mentor yourself! Helping others not only strengthens your network but also builds your own confidence and understanding of the industry. This reciprocal relationship fosters a strong community where everyone can thrive and support one another.

And don't overlook the local scene. Sometimes the most valuable connections are right in your backyard. Local aviation clubs, volunteer organizations, or even just attending community events can lead to enriching relationships. These grassroots connections often open doors to opportunities you didn't even know existed. By surrounding yourself with a diverse network of professionals from all corners of the aviation world, you'll create a strong support system that can help you tackle challenges and celebrate successes together. Every person you meet has something unique to offer. Embrace those connections, learn from their stories, and watch how your career takes off with the help of your expanding network.

Effective Communication and Relationship Building

In the world of aviation, where teamwork is key, effective communication is like the glue that holds everything together. It can make all the difference. Sure, clear communication helps keep things safe and running smoothly, but it goes beyond just sharing information. It's about building trust and mutual respect with your colleagues, clients, and partners. As you navigate career transitions, sharpening your communication skills can help you connect with others on a deeper level, creating a support system that helps you rise in your professional journey.

Aviation is fast-paced, and the stress that comes with it can sometimes throw communication off course. It's hard to be clear when your mind is racing, so managing stress is crucial to staying calm and communicating effectively. Techniques such as mindfulness, deep breathing, and positive affirmations can help you remain focused and present, allowing you to communicate more effectively. When you approach conversations with a calm demeanor, you not only enhance your message but also create a safe space for others to express their thoughts and feelings. It strengthens relationships and builds your confidence as a communicator.

When it comes to building rapport with the various people you interact with, flexibility and empathy are your best friends. Everyone brings their own unique perspective to the table, so being able to adjust your communication style to suit the situation is crucial. Showing that you're open, approachable, and genuinely interested in others' ideas makes it easier to work together to solve problems. Every conversation is a chance to learn something new and strengthen those connections, which is especially helpful during times of career change.

Encouragement plays a huge role in effective communication too. Sharing your experiences and challenges can create a sense of camaraderie, opening the door for others to do the same. Whether it's celebrating a peer's success, lending a supportive ear during tough times, or offering constructive feedback, these moments help build a culture of positivity and motivation. Plus, the relationships you nurture now can become valuable assets as you move forward in your career.

And don't forget the power of the follow-up! After a conversation with a mentor, colleague, or client, a quick check-in can go a long way. It shows you're serious about maintaining the relationship and keeps the communication flowing. By keeping these connections alive, you're not only expanding your support network but also establishing yourself as a reliable and trusted partner in the aviation world.

So, as you continue your career journey, let effective communication and relationship building be the wind beneath your wings, helping you soar toward success and fulfillment!

Chapter 6

Health and Wellness during Transitions

The Importance of Physical Well-Being

Physical well-being is more than just a checkbox on the path to success. It's the foundation, especially in aviation. Whether you're flying the plane, serving in the cabin, or working behind the scenes, staying healthy directly impacts how well you perform, stay safe, and enjoy your work. During those career shifts, it's easy to get caught up in the hustle, but giving some attention to your physical health can give you the edge you didn't know you needed. After all, your body is what gets you from point A to point B in your career, literally and figuratively.

One of the most effective ways to maintain that edge is staying active. No, you don't need to be signing up for marathons, but incorporating some movement into your day is essential. Whether you've been sitting for hours on end or lifting luggage, your body needs a little love. Simple stuff like walking, stretching, or picking up a new hobby like swimming or hiking can boost your energy levels and lift your spirits. It's amazing what a quick walk around the block can do when the day feels like it's dragging on. Plus, staying active keeps you sharp, which can make a huge difference when you're transitioning roles or dealing with the demands of your job.

Now, nutrition. It's easy to grab the quickest snack on the go when you're working unpredictable hours, but the truth is, a little planning goes a long way. Having a balanced meal can change how you feel throughout the day. Think of your meals as refueling for your body; junk food might give you a quick boost, but it's the whole foods that will keep you cruising. Staying hydrated and adding more fruits, veggies, and lean proteins to your diet will make you feel more alert and ready to handle any surprises that come your way. Bonus points for avoiding that mid-afternoon energy crash!

Here's another important point, physical well-being and mental health are teammates in the game of life. The pressure in aviation can be intense, and without a proper outlet, stress can creep up and take the joy out of the work you love. When you stay active, your brain gets a boost of those feel-good chemicals that can help you keep stress at bay. Add in a nutritious diet, and you're setting yourself up for success, both mentally and physically. It's like giving your brain and body the maintenance check they deserve, ensuring they're both in top shape for whatever comes next.

In conclusion, physical health isn't just about avoiding illness or staying in shape for the sake of it, it's about making sure you're ready for whatever life and career transitions throw your way. By keeping fitness, nutrition, and mental health in balance, you're not only preparing yourself for success in the short term but laying the groundwork for long-term fulfillment. As you move forward in your career, remember that taking care of your physical well-being is like upgrading your personal toolkit, making you stronger, sharper, and ready to reach new heights.

Mental Health Strategies for Stress Management

In the fast-paced world of aviation, the demands of flying, handling passengers, and keeping everything on track can feel like juggling a dozen tasks at once. Stress comes in many forms and can take a toll on your physical health, emotional resilience, and overall job satisfaction. It's all a part of the package. Recognizing the signs of stress is the first step toward managing it effectively. By implementing specific mental health strategies, you can navigate the challenges of your career while maintaining a healthy work-life balance.

One powerful way to manage stress is through mindfulness and meditation. These practices help bring you into the present moment, grounding you when everything feels like it's moving a mile a minute. Scheduling a few minutes each day for deep breathing exercises or guided meditation can create a sanctuary of calm amidst the chaos of the aviation industry. Imagine taking a moment to breathe deeply before takeoff or indulging in a quick mindfulness exercise during a layover, these techniques can help reduce anxiety and enhance focus. It's like hitting the reset button for your brain.

Building a support network is another essential strategy. It can feel isolating when stress builds up, but talking things through with fellow aviation professionals, mentors, or even close friends or family can lighten the load. Sharing your experiences or even just venting a little can create connections and make you feel less alone. And if you need more guidance, reaching out to life coaches or mental health professionals can provide tailored advice to help you build resilience and navigate the stress that comes with your role.

Of course, physical health plays a major role in how well you manage stress. It's all connected; exercise, a balanced diet, and good sleep habits can do wonders for your mental well-being. Yes, aviation schedules can be unpredictable, but squeezing in a workout, even if it's just a quick walk or a short routine, can make a huge difference in how you feel. Pair that with nutritious meals and prioritizing sleep, and you'll find your energy levels and mood improve dramatically. A healthy body fuels a healthy mind, giving you the clarity and stamina to tackle each day.

Another key element of stress management is cultivating a positive mindset. It's not about pretending everything's perfect, but rather shifting your perspective. Instead of seeing challenges as roadblocks, try viewing them as chances to grow. Set realistic goals, celebrate small wins, and practice gratitude. It sounds simple, but these habits can change how you approach stressful situations. When you focus on what you can control and approach stress with a proactive mindset, the hurdles become easier to clear.

Finding Balance in Life and Work

When you're so indulged in your work, finding a balance between work and personal life can feel like a constant balancing act. With the unpredictable nature of the industry, it's easy to feel like you're always juggling multiple responsibilities, with no time to catch your breath. Yet, achieving a harmonious balance is not only possible but can also be transformative. By prioritizing your well-being and implementing strategies to manage your time effectively, you can soar to new heights both in your career and personal life.

The first step toward balance is setting clear boundaries. For aviation professionals, this may mean setting specific times for work and personal life, ensuring that one does not encroach upon the other. It is vital to communicate these boundaries to colleagues and family members, fostering an environment where everyone understands the importance of these demarcations. By doing so, you create a structured setting that allows you to focus fully on your responsibilities at work while also dedicating quality time to your loved ones and personal interests.

Time management is your next big ally in finding balance. Tools like planners, digital calendars, or even just setting reminders can help you keep everything on track. Make sure to carve out regular breaks during the workday, even if they're just a few minutes to stretch or clear your mind. These mini-breaks can recharge your energy and improve focus, helping you handle your workload more efficiently without burning out. When you plan your day thoughtfully, it not only boosts productivity but also gives you a better shot at finding moments of peace and calm.

Self-care is non-negotiable when it comes to maintaining balance. It's often the first thing we sacrifice when life gets busy, but taking care of yourself is essential. Whether it's getting regular exercise, engaging in mindfulness practices, or diving into a hobby that you love, carving out time for yourself is important. Remember, self-care isn't a luxury; it's a necessity. When you take care of your physical and mental health, you build resilience and enhance your performance both at work and at home. The energy you invest in yourself pays off in your career and allows you to be present for the people who matter most.

Seek support when needed. Whether it's from life coaches, mentors, or peers, sharing your experiences can provide invaluable insights and encouragement. Connecting with others who understand the unique challenges of your profession can foster a sense of community and belonging. Embrace opportunities for growth and learning, and remember that finding balance is an ongoing journey. By focusing on your well-being and implementing practical strategies, you can navigate the complexities of your career while maintaining a fulfilling and joyful personal life.

Chapter 7

Exploring New Career Paths

Identifying Transferable Skills

Identifying transferable skills is key to unlocking new career opportunities. Each of us has a unique set of abilities that can be applied across a range of industries, but these are often overlooked, especially when thinking about stepping away from traditional aviation roles. Recognizing and being able to clearly communicate these skills can be a game-changer, whether you're a pilot exploring new paths, an aviation agent looking to branch out, or even a parent helping guide your child's career choices.

One of the most valuable and widely transferable skills in aviation is effective communication. Whether you've been a pilot relaying critical updates to air traffic control or a cabin crew member soothing passengers during turbulence, your ability to communicate clearly and professionally is already finely tuned. This skill easily translates to industries like customer service, management, or even coaching, where conveying information in a calm and clear manner is crucial. Think about how your knack for communicating under pressure could make you a standout in industries that thrive on interpersonal skills and empathy.

Problem-solving under pressure is another superpower that aviation professionals bring to the table. In aviation, you're trained to make quick, informed decisions, often when the stakes are high. Whether it's dealing with a technical glitch mid-flight or navigating an unexpected situation with a passenger, you've mastered the art of staying cool while finding solutions. This ability to think on your feet is highly sought after in areas like crisis management, project management, or even entrepreneurial ventures, where quick, strategic thinking is a must.

Leadership is another core skill that can carry you far beyond the aviation industry. As cabin crew and pilots, you have experience leading teams, ensuring safety and compliance, and fostering a positive environment. These leadership skills can translate into opportunities in management, coaching, or even in government roles where guiding teams or initiatives is essential. Your background in aviation shows that you know how to inspire and motivate people, which is a huge asset when exploring new career paths.

Collaboration is a core aspect of aviation, and it's just as important in other industries. Whether in the cockpit or cabin, working closely with others in a high-stakes environment has likely sharpened your teamwork skills. The ability to collaborate effectively with diverse groups of people is valued across all fields, from corporate teams to community projects. When you highlight your experience working harmoniously with others, potential employers or clients will see how you can bring that same energy and cooperative spirit to their team.

Opportunities in Aviation and Beyond

The aviation industry has always been a realm of boundless opportunities, not just for pilots and cabin crew, but for a diverse range of professionals looking to embark on new journeys. As the world gradually recovers from global disruptions, the demand for skilled individuals in aviation is on the rise again. This resurgence offers a chance for parents, agents, and aviation workers to explore diverse career pathways that extend beyond traditional roles. Embracing this shift can lead to fulfilling careers in areas such as aviation management, training, and consultancy, creating a ripple effect that inspires others to pursue their dreams in this dynamic field.

If you're a pilot or part of the cabin crew, transitioning into something new can feel like a leap into the unknown. But think about it, how many jobs out there value leadership, calm communication, and problem-solving under pressure like aviation does? Those skills are your golden ticket to a wide range of industries. Maybe you're interested in aviation safety, or perhaps you've always wanted to start your own business related to travel or logistics. Whatever you choose, those in-air experiences are a strong foundation that can help you shine in any new role.

Now, what about entrepreneurship? If you've ever thought about starting your own venture, the aviation industry is buzzing with opportunities right now. With exciting tech advancements like drones and eco-friendly flying, there's room for big ideas and innovation. Got an idea that could improve safety procedures or enhance the passenger experience? You could be onto something. There's a lot of space for creative solutions, and with the industry evolving so rapidly, being at the forefront of this change could be your game-changer.

Moreover, government officials play a critical role in shaping the aviation sector and ensuring that it thrives. When they invest in infrastructure, education, and workforce programs, they're laying the groundwork for future talent to thrive. But it's a two-way street, connecting with industry leaders and understanding their needs means creating targeted policies that make a real difference. Imagine being part of the conversation that helps bridge the gap between training and real-world opportunities. That's how we ensure the next generation of aviation pros is ready to take flight.

But what about the personal side of things? Career changes can be overwhelming. That's where life coaches and wellness experts come in. Have you ever considered how much easier career transitions can be with a little extra guidance? Coaches can offer practical advice and emotional support to help you manage stress, build confidence, and navigate your next steps with ease. It's like having someone in your corner, making sure you're ready to take on the world with a positive mindset.

Considering Entrepreneurship

Thinking about starting your own business? Considering entrepreneurship can be an exhilarating and rewarding journey. The skills you have developed throughout your career, such as discipline, adaptability, and a keen understanding of team dynamics, translate beautifully into the world of entrepreneurship. And let's face it, entrepreneurship is a chance to take all those unique experiences and turn them into something both personally and financially rewarding.

As someone coming from the aviation world, you've got an edge. You've already navigated high-pressure environments and know how to manage complex situations. This gives you a wealth of knowledge that can be invaluable, especially in niches like life coaching, wellness, or even stress management. By sharing your expertise, you can help others navigate their own career transitions, offering them the guidance and encouragement they need to succeed. The transition from employee to entrepreneur is not just a change in job title; it is a shift in mindset that empowers you to take charge of your destiny.

When considering entrepreneurship, the key is to follow your passion and figure out where you can make the biggest impact. Whether it is guiding others in building confidence and self-esteem or offering stress management strategies, your personal journey can inspire and uplift those around you. Remember, every successful entrepreneur started with a single idea. The trick is to nurture it, fuel your passion, and be willing to take that first step outside your comfort zone. Your aviation background gives you a unique perspective on the needs of your future clients. Use it to your advantage.

Surround yourself with like-minded individuals who share your vision and can provide encouragement along the way. Attend workshops, join professional organizations, or seek mentorship from those who have successfully made the leap. This community can offer invaluable insights and connections that will help you navigate the challenges you face. Collaboration and shared experiences will not only enhance your knowledge but will also reinforce your confidence as you take these bold steps forward.

Ultimately, entrepreneurship is about seeing potential, both in yourself and in your vision for what could be. It's your chance to redefine your career on your own terms, helping others while finding personal fulfillment. The skills and insights you've gained in aviation are your secret weapon. Now's the time to use them to build something great. Remember, every successful entrepreneur started with a bit of uncertainty. But with perseverance, passion, and the right support, you can soar to new heights and make a positive impact on others along the way.

Chapter 8

The Role of Life Coaching in Career Transitions

Understanding Life Coaching Benefits

Life coaching isn't just about career tips and motivational quotes, it's a game changer for personal growth. Think of it as having your own personal cheerleader who's there to help you figure out your goals and strengths while pushing you to be the best version of yourself. When you're working with a life coach, you get more than just advice; you get a real sense of clarity about who you are and where you're headed. It's like finally finding the map in a maze, and trust me, it feels good to know what direction you're going!

One of the best things about life coaching? Confidence. When we're going through big transitions, it's easy to feel like we're walking on shaky ground. A good life coach helps you kick that self-doubt to the curb. They'll guide you to see your own wins (even the small ones) and help you build a positive self-image. The beauty of it? Once you start feeling more confident in your career, that feeling trickles into your personal life, too. Suddenly, you're not just surviving, you're thriving. Whether it's negotiating at work or finally taking up that hobby you've been putting off, you'll have the confidence to dive right in.

Now, let's talk about stress. And not the "I lost my keys" kind, but the "life-is-hitting-me-from-all-sides" type of stress. In aviation, or really any high-pressure job, stress can feel like a constant companion. Professionals in this field often face unique stressors, whether from demanding schedules, safety responsibilities, or the need for impeccable customer service. A life coach can be your secret weapon here, offering you simple but effective stress-busting techniques. Imagine having a mental toolbox full of ways to stay cool, calm, and collected, even when everything seems like it's about to go off the rails. You'll learn to tackle challenges with a sense of resilience that makes you feel like you can handle anything, whether it's a tough day at work or juggling all those "life" things.

Health and wellness coaching is also an integral component of the life coaching experience. You can't really pour from an empty cup, right? And with the busy lives many of us lead, self-care is often the first thing we push to the back burner. A life coach can help you shift that thinking. They'll work with you to create healthier habits, build routines that actually stick, and set goals you can achieve (without feeling like a chore). It's like having a fitness tracker for your overall well-being, reminding you that your health is just as important as everything else on your to-do list.

Ultimately, life coaching is about way more than just figuring out your next career move. It's about finding your groove, managing life's chaos with a smile, and learning to take care of yourself in the process. So why not give it a try? You might just surprise yourself with how much you can grow, both personally and professionally.

Finding the Right Coach for You

If you're convinced that a life coach could be the guidance you need, the next step is finding the right one. It's not a one-size-fits-all kind of deal. Understanding what you need and where you're headed will help you figure out what kind of coaching style clicks with you. Start by taking a moment to reflect on your current situation: Are you in the middle of a career transition? Maybe looking to boost your health and wellness, or even just trying to build some confidence? Being clear on what you want will point you toward the coach who's best suited to help you grow.

When looking for a coach, it's important to consider their background, especially if you're in the aviation industry. It helps to find someone who understands the ins and outs of what pilots, cabin crew, and other aviation professionals go through. You want someone who's got experience in career transition coaching or life coaching and knows how to guide you through the challenges of switching gears. Don't be afraid to ask them about their experience working with people in aviation. After all, it's a huge plus if they already know what kind of journey you're on.

Next up is finding a coaching style that works for you. Some coaches are all about setting goals and creating action plans, while others focus more on emotional support and personal growth. Think about what suits your style better. Do you like a structured approach with clear steps? Or do you prefer a more flexible, go-with-the-flow vibe? A lot of coaches offer introductory sessions or consultations, so take advantage of that to see if their approach feels right. This is your chance to figure out if their style resonates with your needs and if you feel comfortable with how they work.

Another big part of the process is building a good relationship with your coach. Trust, openness, and respect are the foundation here. Pay attention to how you feel when you talk to potential

41

coaches. Do they make you feel heard and understood? Do you get the sense that they're genuinely invested in helping you succeed? A coach who makes you feel confident and pushes you to stretch your limits can have a huge impact on your journey.

Finding the right coach can be life changing, especially if you're going through a career transition. Take the time to find someone who not only fits your professional needs but also aligns with your personal values. With the right support, you'll feel ready to tackle any challenge that comes your way. Invest in yourself now, the rewards of a fulfilling and successful career in aviation are waiting for you.

Setting Expectations for Coaching Sessions

Setting clear expectations for coaching sessions is crucial for getting the most out of your experience, especially if you're navigating big changes in your career. Understanding how coaching works can really help you reach your potential. So, how do you make sure you're making the most of it? Let's break it down.

First off: what's your goal? This is your journey, so it's important to have a clear idea of your goals before stepping into a session. Are you looking to boost your confidence? Manage stress more effectively? Improve your communication skills? Whatever your goals may be, think about them in specific terms. This gives your coach a roadmap to follow, and more importantly, it gives *you* a clear target to aim for. What's the one thing you'd like to tackle right away?

Next up, how often should you meet with your coach? Weekly? Bi-weekly? It's all about finding the rhythm that works for you. Establishing a consistent schedule helps keep the momentum going and ensures you're actively working towards your goals.

Think of it like this: each session is a checkpoint where you can pause, reflect on your progress, and tweak your approach if needed. Have you thought about how much time you can dedicate to this? Setting a timeline helps make sure you stay on track.

One thing that's often overlooked is the importance of the coach-client relationship. Coaching isn't just about sitting back and receiving advice, it's a partnership. You bring your goals, your experiences, and your willingness to grow, and your coach brings the tools and guidance to help you along the way. But here's the catch: the real work happens on your end. Are you ready to dive in and embrace the process? It requires trust, openness, and a bit of vulnerability. Your coach will guide you, but ultimately, *you* are the one steering the ship.

Now, let's talk about something that's super important: managing your expectations. Personal growth doesn't happen overnight. Some sessions will feel like major breakthroughs, while others might feel more like small steps forward and that's okay! Progress isn't always a straight line. Have you been patient with yourself lately? Celebrating small wins along the way helps keep the momentum going and reminds you that every step counts, no matter how small. So, if things feel slow at times, remember: you're building something that lasts. Your transformation will unfold at its own pace, and that's what makes it so powerful.

Chapter 9

Success Stories and Case Studies

Inspiring Journeys of Former Pilots

The journeys of former pilots are proof that the sky is just the starting point. For many, stepping away from the cockpit isn't about leaving their passion for flying behind but about discovering new ways to soar. These stories of transition highlight resilience, adaptability, and the courage to face new challenges head-on. By embracing change, former pilots not only find fulfillment in different careers but also inspire others to chase their dreams with confidence.

Take, for example, the story of one former airline pilot who transitioned into life coaching. After years of navigating the complexities of air travel, he discovered a passion for helping others navigate their life journeys. This transition was not without its hurdles, yet his background in aviation provided him with a unique perspective on overcoming obstacles. By applying the same principles of discipline and focus that kept him safe in the cockpit, he now empowers individuals to soar in their personal and professional lives, proving that the skills learned in aviation can translate into meaningful support for others.

Similarly, another pilot turned entrepreneur found success in the wellness industry, creating a business that emphasizes stress management and self-care. This journey began with a recognition of the mental and physical demands of flying, which often lead to burnout. By channeling her experience into developing holistic wellness programs, she has helped countless individuals find balance and health in their lives. Her story serves as a beacon of hope for those struggling with stress, demonstrating that a passion for well-being can emerge from the rigorous demands of a flying career.

The inspiring journeys of these former pilots illustrate the importance of confidence and self-esteem during career transitions. With the right mindset and support, individuals can break free from the confines of their previous roles and explore new horizons. Each story reflects a common theme: the belief that one's skills are transferable and can lead to success in various fields. Parents, aviation professionals, and government officials can take heart in these narratives, knowing that career changes can lead to fulfilling and impactful new paths.

At the heart of these pilots' journeys is the realization that the aviation world isn't just about flying; it's about the people, the connections, and the lives they've touched along the way. These inspiring stories encourage everyone, from pilots to cabin crew and beyond, to embrace change and pursue their passions. By sharing their experiences, former pilots not only redefine their own lives but also inspire others to explore the vast possibilities that await them in their unique journeys.

Cabin Crew Transitions: Stories of Resilience

In the world of aviation, career transitions can be both thrilling and nerve-wracking, especially for cabin crew members who often face significant changes in their lives. Yet, it's the stories of resilience among these professionals that truly highlight the strength of the human spirit. These journeys reveal not only the challenges that come with career shifts but also the creative ways people find to rise above them. Through these stories, others are inspired to face change with confidence, knowing that they aren't navigating this path alone.

One such story is that of Sarah, a former flight attendant who found herself at a crossroads after an unexpected layoff. Rather than allowing this setback to deter her, Sarah chose to view it as an opportunity for growth. With the support of a career transition coach, she explored her passions beyond aviation. She discovered a love for health and wellness that had long been overshadowed by her flying duties. By pursuing further education in this field, Sarah not only rebuilt her career but also empowered others to lead healthier lives, proving that resilience can pave the way for new and fulfilling paths.

Then there's David, who shifted from cabin crew to aviation consultancy. After years of serving passengers, David realized he had a wealth of knowledge about customer service and operational efficiency. With encouragement from his peers and a mentor in the industry, he took the leap into consultancy, where he now helps airlines enhance their service quality. His story exemplifies how skills gained in one role can be transferable to another, reinforcing the notion that cabin crew members possess a unique set of talents that are valuable in various contexts.

Of course, these transitions aren't just about the professional shift. It's also about navigating the emotional side of change. Many cabin crew members have found solace in connecting with one another, sharing experiences, and providing encouragement through mentorship programs. This collaborative spirit not only fosters a sense of belonging but also cultivates confidence and self-esteem among individuals who may be feeling lost in their transition. By leaning on each other, they build a network of support that becomes essential during times of change.

Ultimately, the narratives of cabin crew transitions serve as a beacon of hope for all those facing career shifts. They remind us that resilience is not merely about enduring hardships but also about thriving in the face of them. Each story reinforces the idea that with the right mindset, support, and resources, anyone can soar to new heights, transforming their careers and lives in the process. As we celebrate these journeys, we encourage others to embrace their own transitions with courage and optimism, knowing that they, too, can write their own remarkable stories of resilience.

Entrepreneurs Who Soared After Aviation

Many individuals who have soared through the skies in aviation have discovered that their experiences as pilots and cabin crew can serve as a launchpad for thriving entrepreneurial ventures. The skills developed in this industry, such as adaptability, leadership, and problem-solving, translate seamlessly into the business world. These entrepreneurs not only embraced their passion for flight but also leveraged their unique insights and experiences to carve out successful paths in various industries. Their journeys remind us that the sky is not the limit; it is merely the beginning of new horizons.

One inspiring example is a former airline pilot who transitioned into a life coaching business. Drawing on the challenges faced in the cockpit, this entrepreneur created a coaching framework that helps clients navigate life changes with confidence and resilience. By utilizing stress management techniques honed during turbulent flights, they empower clients to overcome personal and professional obstacles. This transition not only provided a fulfilling career but also allowed the pilot to give back to the community by mentoring others who may be struggling with their own transitions.

Then there's the story of a cabin crew member who used her extensive travel background to create a wellness coaching practice. After spending years dealing with the physical and mental demands of constant travel, she realized how crucial balance and self-care are for professionals on the go. By combining her passion for health and wellness with the insights gained from her aviation career, she created tailored programs that help busy professionals maintain balance and well-being. Her journey illustrates how the knowledge gained in aviation can inspire innovative solutions that serve a broader audience.

The entrepreneurial spirit also thrives in those who shifted from aviation management roles to consultancy. A former airport operations manager utilized her experience in logistics and team coordination to advise businesses on improving operational efficiency. Her expertise in managing high-pressure environments translated into valuable strategies for companies looking to enhance their performance. This transition not only fulfilled her ambitions but also positioned her as a trusted advisor in the corporate world, proving that the skills gained in aviation are highly sought after in various sectors.

As these entrepreneurs demonstrate, the lessons learned in aviation extend far beyond the cockpit. They embody resilience, creativity, and the willingness to adapt, qualities that are essential for success in any entrepreneurial endeavor. Their stories serve as a reminder to pilots, cabin crew, and aviation workers that embarking on a new journey can lead to incredible opportunities. The experiences gathered in aviation are not just memories; they are the foundation for building new dreams and soaring to new heights in the world of business.

Chapter 10

Taking Action and Moving Forward

Committing to Your Transition Plan

Fully committing to your transition plan is essential when facing the often challenging shift from one phase of your career to another. Whether you are a pilot, cabin crew member, or aviation worker, the decision to change your career path is a courageous one that requires dedication and clarity of purpose. By fully committing to your plan, you set the stage for achieving your goals and realizing your potential. Embrace this commitment as an opportunity to redefine your career path while reinforcing your self-worth and capabilities.

To stay committed, it's crucial to set clear, actionable goals within your transition plan. Break your objectives into manageable milestones that allow you to monitor your progress and celebrate small wins along the way. These milestones not only highlight your strengths but also reinforce your drive to succeed. Keep in mind that every step forward, no matter how small, moves you closer to your ultimate aspirations and boosts your self-confidence.

In the process of committing, you may encounter challenges that test your resolve. Stress and doubt can creep in, especially during times of uncertainty. This is where effective stress management techniques come into play. Incorporating mindfulness practices, physical well-being routines, and support from life coaches can help you navigate these obstacles. Remember that facing challenges is part of the journey; it is through overcoming these hurdles that you will find strength and resilience.

Building a supportive network is essential for staying committed to your goals. Engage with mentors, peers, and industry professionals who can provide guidance and encouragement. Whether through formal coaching or informal conversations, these connections can offer valuable insights and foster a sense of accountability. Sharing your journey with others not only enhances your motivation but also reinforces the idea that you are not alone in this situation.

In the end, committing to your plan is about having confidence in yourself and your ability to grow. Embrace the uncertainty as a gateway to new opportunities, knowing that every pilot and cabin crew member has faced their own career transitions. With a well-thought-out plan, the right support, and an unwavering belief in your abilities, you can soar to new heights in your career. Your journey is uniquely yours, and your commitment to it will shape the future you desire.

Embracing Change and Uncertainty

Change can be tough. It's like trying to find your way through turbulence when you're hoping for smooth skies. But, if there's one thing you know from being in aviation, it's that change is inevitable, and embracing it can open up doors you didn't even know were there. Whether it's new technology, shifting regulations, or just the ever-changing world of passenger demands, staying flexible is the key to not only surviving but thriving in this industry. And guess what? The same applies when you're making a big career shift.

The first thing to remember when facing change is that it's totally normal to feel all kinds of emotions: anxiety, doubt, even a bit of excitement. You're human, after all! Instead of letting those feelings paralyze you, acknowledge them. Think back to times in your career when you've faced the unknown (because, let's be real, there have been plenty of those) and remind yourself that you got through it. You've already proven to yourself that you can navigate tricky situations. If you can handle an emergency landing or a cranky passenger at 35,000 feet, you can handle this.

As you explore new avenues in your career, consider the value of adaptability. This industry thrives on professionals who can make quick decisions, solve problems on the fly, and collaborate in fast-paced environments. These same qualities will serve you well in whatever new venture you pursue. Being open to change allows you to pivot when opportunities arise, or when unexpected challenges pop up. Think of adaptability not just as a skill, but as a superpower you've sharpened through years in aviation. Use it to embrace the twists and turns of your career shift with confidence.

Support is another crucial element in embracing change. Surround yourself with a network of individuals who inspire and uplift you. This community may include fellow aviation professionals, mentors, or coaches specializing in career transition and personal development. Engaging in open conversations about your fears and aspirations can help alleviate the burden of uncertainty. These connections provide not only encouragement but also valuable insights that can guide you through your journey. Remember, you are not alone in this transition; many have walked this path and are eager to share their experiences with you.

In the end, try to shift your perspective on uncertainty. What if, instead of seeing uncertainty as something scary, you start seeing it as a door to new possibilities? Every unknown is an opportunity for growth, new skills, and maybe even discovering something about yourself you didn't know. Approach this next step with curiosity. What can you learn? What strengths can you uncover? This career shift doesn't have to feel like a leap into the abyss, it can be the start of an adventure where you're in the captain's seat, charting a new course for yourself.

Staying Motivated on Your Journey

As you come to the end of this journey, whether it's through the pages of this book or the transition in your career, one thing is clear: staying motivated is what will carry you through. Change, especially in a field like aviation, can feel overwhelming at times. However, maintaining motivation is crucial to achieving your goals and soaring to new heights. Embracing a mindset of resilience and positivity will help you overcome obstacles and keep your ambitions alive, even when the road gets rough.

One effective way to stay motivated is to set clear, achievable goals. Breaking your larger aspirations into smaller, manageable milestones can provide a sense of direction and make the journey feel less overwhelming. Each time you reach a milestone, take a moment to celebrate your progress. This practice not only boosts your confidence but also reinforces your commitment to your career transition. Remember, every small step takes you closer to your ultimate destination, so acknowledge and appreciate the journey along the way.

Surrounding yourself with a supportive network can also greatly enhance your motivation. Engage with fellow aviation professionals, mentors, or life coaches who understand the unique challenges you may face. Sharing your experiences and learning from others can provide invaluable insights and encouragement. Additionally, having a solid support system can help you stay accountable to your goals and remind you of your capabilities during challenging times. Remember, you are not alone on this journey; there are many who are eager to support you.

Incorporating positive affirmations and visualization techniques into your daily routine can be a powerful tool for maintaining motivation. Visualize yourself achieving your career goals and living your dream. This mental imagery can boost your confidence and inspire you to take action. Pair this with positive affirmations that reinforce your strengths and potential. By regularly affirming your abilities and envisioning your success, you create a mindset that empowers you to face challenges with determination and enthusiasm.

And finally, don't forget to take care of yourself. The journey to a new career or life path can be mentally and physically demanding. Prioritize your well-being, whether that's through exercise, mindfulness, or simply giving yourself the time to recharge. The better you feel, the more energy you'll have to keep pushing forward. You're no good to yourself or your goals if you're running on empty, so treat your health as the most important co-pilot on this journey.

As we wrap up, remember that the most important part of any journey, whether in aviation or life, isn't just the destination, but the ride itself. Stay motivated, stay committed, and take time to enjoy each part of the process. The skies ahead are wide open, and your next adventure is waiting.